THE TRACK

WRITTEN BY: VERNA LYNNE REESE
ILLUSTRATED BY KAMAL RENELLE LEWIS

AuthorHouse™
1663 Liberty Drive
Bloomington, IN 47403
www.authorhouse.com
Phone: 1 (800) 839-8640

Published by AuthorHouse 07/10/2018

ISBN: 978-1-5462-4927-6 (sc)
ISBN: 978-1-5462-4928-3 (e)

Library of Congress Control Number: 2018907992

Print information available on the last page.

This book is printed on acid-free paper.

authorHOUSE®

The Track

by Verna Lynne Reese

You may think I'm slow but there's something you don't know.

I have a reason during track season and it helps my ego grow.

So, go ahead, run as fast as you can.

And as you all soar and the crowd roars...

You won't know exactly who they're cheering for.

But as for me, I take my time getting to the finish line.

So, when I come around there's no one else to see.

And I can be sure...

...the crowd is
cheering just for me!

THE TRACK

You may think I'm slow
But there's something you don't know
I have a reason during track season
And it helps my ego grow
So go ahead, run as fast as you can
And as you all soar
and the crowd roars
You wont know exactly who they're
cheering for
But as for me,
I take my time getting to the finish line
So when I come around
There's no one else to see
And I can be sure
The crowd is cheering just for me

Lightning Source UK Ltd.
Milton Keynes UK
UKHW05f1314310718
326549UK00006B/77/P